 Cover art from Monet's "Garden Path, Giverny". Design by Scars Publications. ISBN 1-891470-43-4. For further information and to order books visit JanineCanan.com.

Many of these works were previously published in the following publications.

Books by Janine Canan: *Changing Woman* (Scars: Chicago IL, 2000). *Star in My Forehead: Selected Poems by Else Lasker-Schüler* (Holy Cow!: Duluth MN, 2000). *Love, Enter* (Open Bone: Port Angeles WA, 1998). *Goddess Poems* (Sagittarius: Port Townsend WA, 1997). *Her Magnificent Body, New & Selected Poems* (Manroot: San Francisco CA, 1986). *Shapes of Self* (Emily Dickinson: Berkeley CA, 1982). *Daughter,* illustr. by Donna Brookman (Emily Dickinson: Berkeley CA, 1981). *Who Buried the Breast of Dreams* (Emily Dickinson: Berkeley CA, 1981). *The Hunger* (Oyez: Berkeley CA, 1979). *Of Your Seed* (Oyez: Berkeley CA, 1977).

Anthologies: *Contemporary Authors, # 181,* ed. Joyce Nakamura (Gale: Farmington Hills MI, 1999). *Get Well Wishes: Prayers and Poems to Wish You Well,* ed. June Cotner (Harper: San Francisco CA, 2000). *Her Words,* ed. Burleigh Muten (Shambhala: Boston MA, 1999). *Return of the Goddess Engagement Calendar,* ed. Burleigh Muten (Stewart, Tabori, Chang: New York NY, 1999). *To Honor A Teacher,* ed. Jeffrey Spoden (Andrews McMeel: Kansas City MO, 1999). *We'Moon Gaia Calendar,* ed. Musawa (Mother Tongue Ink: Estacada OR, 1994, 1998, 1999). *From the Realm of the Ancestors: Essays in Honor of Marija Gimbutas,* ed. Joan Marler (Knowledge Ideas & Trends: Manchester CT, 1997). *It's All The Rage! Poems About Suicide and Its Alternatives* (Andrew Mountain: Hartford CT, 1997). *Least Loved Beasts of the Really Wild West,* ed. Terril and Yvette Shorb (Native West: Prescott AZ, 1997). *Prayers to Protest: Poems that Center and Bless Us,* ed. Jennifer Bosveld (Pudding House: Johnstown OH, 1997). *Hard Love: Writings on Intimacy and Violence,* ed. Elizabeth Claman (Queen of Swords: Eugene OR, 1996). *Collected Poems: Marrowstone Poets and Friends,* ed. Pat Britt and Gwen Moore (Turtle Press: Marrowstone WA, 1995). *She Rises like the Sun: Invocations of the Goddess by Contemporary American Women Poets,* ed. Janine Canan (The Crossing: Freedom CA, 1989). *Up Late: American Poetry Since 1970,* ed. Andrei Codrescu (Four Walls Eight Windows: New York NY, 1987). *State of Peace: The Women Speak,* ed. Natasha Borovsky, Florence Miller, Mary Rudge & Elaine Starkman (Gull Books, New York NY, 1987). *New Lesbian Writing: An Anthology,* ed. Margaret Cruikshank (Grey Fox: San Francisco CA, 1984). *Women Poets of the World,* ed. Joanna Bankier and Dierdre Lashgari (Macmillan: New York NY, 1983). *New England Poetry Engagement Book 1983,* ed. Eric Linder and Paul Marion (Yellow Umbrella: Chatham MA, 1982).

Journals: *The Acorn, Along the Path, Alternative Harmonies, Aporia, Arnazella Arts & Literary Magazine, The Aurorean, Berkeley Works, The Bloomsbury Review, Caprice, Children Churches & Daddies, Collage: Sonoma Valley Arts, Colorado North Review, Color Wheel, The Creative Woman Quarterly, The Cypress Review, Day Tonight Night Today, Deepest Valley Review, Exquisite Corpse, Focus, Free Verse, The Gentle Survivalist, Goddessing, Heart & Wings, Kalliope, Kavindra, The Kore, The Laureate Letter, Luna, Minotaur, Mosaic, Multiples, Pandora, Pangolin Papers, Phoenix Rising, Rebirth of Artemis, Red Coral, Surprise Me, Temenos, Thesmophoria, Tight, Visions, West Wind Review, A Wise Woman's Garden,* and *Writer's Gazette.*

Recordings: *Janine Canan Reads,* audio cassette (Heaven Productions: Berkeley CA, 1991). *Torture and Triumph: Scars Collection,* compact disc (Scars: Chicago IL, 2001).

For you, dear Reader

Poems belong to those who need them,
not those who write them.
—Antonio Skarmeta

INTRODUCTION

Janine Canan is a poet of questing imagination and seemingly endless originality. For over thirty years her poetry has appeared in magazines, anthologies, and in her ten published collections, beginning in 1977 with *Of Your Seed* (Oyez: Berkeley) and ending with her incomparable *Changing Woman* (Scars: Chicago, 2000).

Now with the publication of *In the Palace of Creation*, her readers can for the first time experience the full range of her poetry in a single collection. Wisely selected by poet and editor Susan Hahn, the poems in this volume bear witness to the evolution of Canan's creative voice from 1969 to 1999.

Here the reader will find simple poems like "Before the Storm" which testify to Canan's enduring love of nature; metaphorically complex poems like "The Abandoned Garden" which are both erotic and sorrowful; poems like "Wild Music," modeled after the lyrics of the great Hindu mystical poet Mirabai, which reveal the most intimate depths of Canan's spiritual life; and poems like "At the Vulva Stone," written to the Great Goddess and ardently feminist while never ceasing to be sensuous and lyrical.

Canan has been influenced by Sappho, Emily Dickinson, Anna Akhmatova, Carolyn Kizer, and Denise Levertov. The reader will find poems to all of them here as well as Canan's translations of poems by Else Lasker-Schüler, Marguerite Yourcenar, and Mirabai.

This is an unusually rich collection. Perhaps Canan herself best captures the spirit of it when she says in her long prose meditation "A Good Laugh": "Beauty is created constantly everywhere . . . The whole is a splendid vast writhing joyous and suffering Serpent, shedding her skin as She wiggles along, perpetually revealing a new Self that rises out of her own pure delight."

Mary Mackey

CONTENTS

I. EARTH TALKS

II. SOMEONE STEPS NEAR

III. Moving Together in This Conversation

IV. Elements of Love

V. THE SOUND OF CHANGE

VI. NATURAL TRAVELERS

VII. IN OTHER WORDS (TRANSLATIONS)

VIII. In the Palace of Creation

Wherever Thou leadest me,
it is Thou, the same,
the one companion of my endless life.
—Tagore

1. EARTH TALKS

Abandoned Garden

In front we planted purple periwinkle stars
that sprawled under heavenly bamboo
around two towering pines.
Over the fence came escallonia's rosy blooms.

Then the hillside steeply declined:
Along the steps cheery marguerites,
shy coral bells you planted on your knees,
then the ruffled, puffed-up, proud red rhodies.

In the corner anemones floated their clouds of silk.
In the window box, fluorescent pink and fiery red,
madly muttering impatiens
I watered with my tears.

By the pale blue door, azaleas bled
on the silent horrified rose.
Near the hostile mailbox, the young dogwood
never dared bloom her tender pink.

The infected maple struggled to spread her roots.
On the meadow wildflowers multiplied
in a thick green carpet where we might have lain
tucked in each other's blossoming hearts.

Two Eagles

Below the mountain white and solitary
we stretch out on the emerald hill
and empty our bottle of flowery champagne.

As we walk the watery shore we see
high upon the cliff on the upper branch of a fir
two eagles big as humans.

She's shy, you say as yards of black wing
unfold across the sky, and he turns his large white
gold-beaked head to watch her fly.

By Morning

I've been mapping out the roads, going on foot. Scruffy woods, low brush, and a sticky view that doesn't go far. But I've been going round the land, marking down the paths, getting the general shape of the place. I especially like the hills' huge grassy thighs, dry and well worth mounting. Upon them I can see the sky's long restful line. And when at night the sun goes below, I alone crawl down their side and prowl across the land, out to that secret thing lying like a crushed skull in the middle of the landscape—a crater filled with dark. There I crouch and stare, at that socket that stares back as if it will never stop asking questions. Later I am invited into the depths of the cavern, where the teeth are hung—hammered and finely tooled copper, gold and silver. I am not scared and wind back out to the road by morning.

At the Vulva Stone

The birds loudly love
the Goddess' ancient temple.
So do the tiny daisies
crowding the grass.
The sun pokes his tired old nose
through the clouds
to see her grand and intimate stones.
A young man building muscle
jogs past the crevice
where her child crowns.
And one wild sparrow lands
rocking onto her lush green mound,
drunkenly dancing.

Forever

Magnolia tree, knotted and scrawny, flame bud, rose bud, wild yellow iris. Hands reaching deep in the soil. Or waiting curled, purring in your lap's dark meadow. Gold ring of laughter. Companion of my dreams. An aureole dances around your skin's darkness: It is a wish. Sacred your eyes open as I enter in. Then we sleep together, dream and stir, braiding our silken limbs longer and longer. We are growing in the yard. At night we're lit by the stars. White fur of magnolia, flame red of rose, mouths of yellow iris. Fingers that link, necks listening in the wind. Two wishes that have understood one another forever.

Forest Temple

The forests are falling,
rolling down the hills like tears.
Beyond these cemeteries the last firs
draw back shuddering.

Oh deeper I must go to find
that temple where the kinglets chime,
guarded by an elk priest
whose beard flows along fern carpet.

In greeny gold of the first cathedral
earth grows long and slow.
Black birds glide through mossy arches
past thousand-year-old spruces.

High upon the hemlock tower
a red-crested woodpecker drums.
Kneeling inside her fragrant heart
I exhale her radiant light.

Knowledge

What do the poppies,
lithe dancers in the light,
know of the stem?

To them, the hairy hardy
water-bearer below
seems primitive.

Yet beyond
their red silk flags
lies a land more splendorous still.

Stubborn Rose

The peacock's scream
floods the valley
as he draws his long blue and gold tail
over the bright green grass.

*

Night descends on the howling earth.
Where the guardians once stood—
elderberry, fir, cedar and spruce—
day gapes.

*

The gray-haired woman
painstakingly
paints rose cream
on her vanishing mouth.

*

Honored heron on your rock,
can you tell me what o'clock?
Is it time to hurry home
or may I watch you stare at Rome?

*

There!
Like a ladybug I rise
up through azure dusk
into her whirling white Eye.

*

Stubborn rose,
straining against the ripping winds
you splay your last pink bud
wide open to the light.

Snowfall

Fat little junco
in black silk hood
stuffs from thistle feeder,
dangling under snow-covered eaves.

While flakes
flutter from feather heaven,
skiing the edge of wind,
thudding off bushy cedar's burdened limbs.

Behind my window I step
too close—and away he flies.
Yielding my pen to glories of white—
he returns to feast under the flowing skies.

Awakening

I
The world is a baby
wrapped in the gauzy fog.
Waves lap the shore,
a million tender voices babbling.
Afar, the lonely horn booms.

II
Walking past the house
a brown-haired girl pulls on her gloves.
Frost hovers on the roseless hedge.
Mercury street lamps stain morning pink.
Crows tumble to the pearly grass.

III
Waves shrug their shoulders
against the sand.
A lone gull stands on a boulder
sunk deep in the strait.
The sky is a magnificence of blues
and grays and whites.
Bent over the bluff an old fir
waits for the wind.
Tentative raindrops stroke my face
and the gull cries.

IV

Crows stomp the roof.
Morning stretches all the way to night,
third eye flaring.
All the birds come out to praise.
Cars insecure, territorial, growl back.
Cows bury their noses in the endless lawn
where dreams are woven.
And baby moon plays peek-a-boo
in the palace of the fir.

Before the Storm

Two orioles perch on a telephone wire
over a grassy field of oleanders, whistling.
Workers listen to songs on the radio.

The mountains bend close
to find out what the humans are up to.
Birdlings tumble into bursting yellow blooms.

A broad black bird sails down valley.
On the highest hill towers the temple
of the Lord the whole world bows down to—

except one woman, who pauses on the lower steps
surveying the landscape, and above her
the slow-moving darkening clouds.

Radioactive

Amchitka,
Bikini,
Bosnia,
Chernobyl,
Eniwetok,
Hanford,
Hiroshima,
Iraq,
Jorñada del Muerte,
Kosovo,
Meralinga,
Nagasaki,
Pakistan,
Palomares,
Pit Nine,
Rajastan,
San Francisco Bay,
Savannah River,
Shoshone Nevada,
Spokane Reservation,
Tahiti,
Three Mile Island—

radioactive forever.
The feminization
of everything
is required.

Jay Joy

Blue jay is back,
shaking her shiny black crest,
climbing the fir tree
branch by branch,
past the conquering crow
all the way to the radiant crown
where she leaps
into pure blue light.

Earth Talks

Beneath the spongy wet grass
the stream talks to me.
Conversations among tall trees
swirl through my hair.
The full moon whispers
behind my back.

My caged heart whines
and my dog lies down panting.
All night Earth babbles
her incessant stream.
The fearful disappear—
there is no one but us.

Waves

As I walk the wet sand
watching for northern lights,
the sun gone,
my white dog a search-light,
waves clapping in the wind,
all the teary voices rush into my ears
and my hair whips in the night.

Everything they tell me.
I go deeper in the suffering
and am flooded with the meaning,
foam feet running toward mine.
The lights come on, of the city we are building.
My white dog waves her plumy tail
and stars appear.

Cold invades my heart with love.
Alive, they say, *alive.*
My white dog sits and she hears too.
We are all waves—
roiling and whispering,
daring and retreating
and once more daring to love.

Flight

Clouds heaped like egg whites, pinked by the western sun. Grand canyons of clouds on an endless slate-blue ocean. Golden rose cliffs tumble down to the sea, fade to dusky pink and gray. Airplane passengers, knowing conspirators, smile over expanding azure seas. At the horizon cloud banks veil the approach. Surging white clouds—racing messengers of light—rush forward like friends to greet us. And a mysterious swathe of peach-streaked sunlit being passes by. Scorching tower of dazzling light! Impenetrable solid gray washed in a pink that dilutes and floods the whole sky.

Paradise opens upon an earthly landscape. Under fuchsia sky the wide aqua sea crests with foam as we fly westward into light, through time and life suffused with more and more glory — in a dream where civilization is imagination and beauty becomes reality. Oh beauty, gateway to the Goddess realm, heart's finest dream, mauve known Now. This fading dream offering diaphanous passage to where? Oh happiness, oh gratitude, dimming unto night. This pale evening in Cloudland, where sleeping hearts yearn on toward the East.

Night. Beauteous arm of Snow Queen rises slowly over the Arctic world. Cool night is coming. Where, where, pale place? Life, what are you? Dim blue vault, clouded seas, rose crest continuing. The Journey—onward, onward—space—clarity—vast stretches—obscurity—nowhere—enveloping—impatient—incertitude—no answer—never—all that was hoped—gone—continuing—coming—more—so plain—and fades. Little dreams of clouds scattered over the sea.

Mother long lost, millennial Mother—I'm flying home.

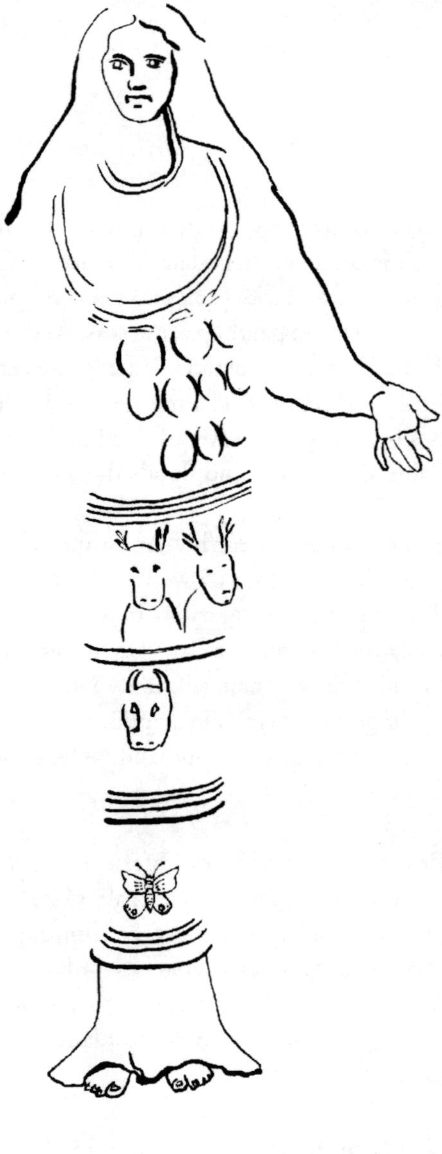

11. SOMEONE STEPS NEAR

Woman

In the bright light
at the typewriter
I try to tell you
how I remember you.
Sudden lightning
strikes me and my mind
pours down rain.
Wet cars stream
down Grove Street
allowing occasional
silence to think.
In the city your face
is a dream—of dahlias,
fuchsias and dense
summer begonias, I wrote
years ago, my feelings
a jungle of desires.
Delicate plum blossoms,
golden doronicums,
starry flowers of the dogwood,
swollen eager buds of the lilac and
mountain ash, you answered me,
your young face aged and thinner,
your body of children
bent in dream, oh
your perfect petal skin
radiant as the sun
when you laughed back heartily
as an ocean wave. I remember

you saying, I like to be
at the very edge, drawn up
defiant like a child
waiting for the waves to crash.
You wanted to be drowned and
remain safe—now survival thorns
surround your soft yellow petals
as they slowly open their
fragile secrets of the moon.
Night-blooming cactus,
store of sun and rain,
frail easy flower, so lavishly
opening, practical plant,
so concisely closed—how can I
tell you what you seem.
The night is wet
and the images blur
and glow in my mind
aflame.

The Sea

A poet is a poet at birth, before,
claims Elli, driving the coast of Crete,
even when not writing she feels
more strongly and deeply.
Sun, pounding on asphalt, flashes on the sea.

*

Couples chat in the bright cafes,
lanterns swing under starlight,
deep blue disappearing behind them,
empty roads, the water's edge barely visible,
a thin white lip of foam.

*

Wandering uphill past strangers,
white-washed houses, blue-trimmed windows,
I smell the sweet sharp scent and follow,
heart surging to cliff's edge
where rock gives way to transparent sea.

In December

In December when the day sucks dark,
in the crawling slit of time,
I fell asleep on a starlit field.

Snowy fingers poked me but I
sank deeper into my desire
for once to meet the night.

Little fires inside warmed me,
though the wind blew cold
as a warning voice.

But how I longed for the night,
her secret subtle cheek, her opening mouth,
her wet tongue.

My fires flared as the hillside
curved before my eyes
into a silk sleeve or a soft breast.

My heart sighed as I sank
ever deeper into this surprising dream,
and snuggling up to her back,

my right hand that took so long
to grow strong melted round the moon—
I slept on.

Creation (Part 1)

Twelve years old, I lie awake in my bed. How far does the sky go—the dark, the stars arcing over my head? Something moves forward I can't take back to Mother or Father. And what I carry on will not return to me. Stars appear through the ceiling. Shadows move restlessly. The avocado's large hands reach in through the window. The house echoes inside me. Mother roams darkly from floor to floor. Father passes through, opening windows. He wants to throw out the old things, the unused. I fear for my doll, the quilt that Grandmother made, the hand-rolled pillow embroidered with blue. I tell him *No.* I leave home.

Your Pictures

I
You find yourself
each winter—as you
take that bend—
in the great oak
leafless dreaming,
in the beam of your headlight.

All your pictures—
the ones you didn't take—
left behind you
at every turn of the road
you chose.

II
Mother,
stepping onto the boat—
you watch,
eyes brimming,
as she turns and waves.

III
Two years old—
plumper
than you remembered—
next to your brother
of thick yellow cream.

You'd already learned
the habit of sadness.

IV
You take hurt hard.
Two stones
on the dining table—
smooth, earth-journeyed, scarred.
Inedible
as thin green milk,
flat as two ungrown breasts,
cold, insensate as angry mother—
unforgiven, unmourned.

V
Julie,
austere in light-planes
that barely separate her
from you—
daughter still
though fought
three thousand miles away.

VI
Sitting by the violins
in your burgundy dress,
your hair done up in braids,
your eyes gaze up to the balcony—
his eyes are looking down.
Your eyes gaze up to the balcony—
his eyes look down.

VII
Denise,
leaning by the window,
her breasts two light-pears,
fingers your silver—
belly of moon.

VIII
I step in the light
and snap you—
head thrown back
in a sudsy bath,
laughter rinsing you
down to the bone.

IX
You,
holding a glass of sweet vermouth,
kneel before the fire,
carrots, celery, purple cabbage
in your lap,
cheeks still flushed from the bath,
your hair wet, your knees bare,
and all around you
the red red robe.

X
The Hudson is frozen.
Train cars sleep by the tracks.
I stand by the window,
behind me the white
smoothly made bed,
my knees against the heater,
a cold quartz stone in my hand.

XI
Old Oak,
eye now closed for winter
that silently braids
your dream—
when the mists fall
you are there,
when the rains fall
you are there,
when the snows fall
you are there,

whenever someone steps near.

Irene and Me

I'm waiting patiently
for an immaculate conception—
though I found out long ago,
though I found out the moment I met light,
there are no immaculate conceptions.

And yet there's Irene
in her neat plaid wool skirt, a red
or blue blouse, a perfectly drawn line on each lid—
her glasses never tilt, her smile never fails,
and when she's finished, she leaves.

And though she's childless—
how could a child fit in that slim skirt—
she conceives herself immaculately each day,
a warm new baby with clean baby skin
and eager baby feet.

But I'm waiting and waiting for the day
when I arrive on time, scrubbed
and dressed the way I looked the day before,
knowing tomorrow no birth pangs, no blood,
only the me I conceived.

Old Lullaby

In this frame I only want to listen to Bach. I am a fine poet and can only write fine poems, I am a good friend and can only love my friends, I am a good doctor, my patients can only grow more whole. I am larger than I imagined I was—we spoke of it together, our eyes large as a child's. Emotions fueling feelings that stand outside us, watch over us like clear midnight skies, the Milky Way, Greek marbles painted in color—terra-cotta arms, azure blue eyes. We live by the sea and the sky, dreaming it, drinking it, singing it as an old lullaby, telling it as a bedtime story, the last words on our lips before we die. We wait for it. We wade in it—so clear—over these pebbles into the sand.

Dear Body

Dear Body, gazing in the mirror it is you
that I behold with thankfulness.
You have been faithful these forty years.
With only a sore knee at puberty, some intestinal
rumblings before authority and teary outpourings
in the face of love, have you occasionally
asserted independence, disapproval, disregard of me.

Nor can I seriously object to the lines in your brow
that reveal where I have been thinking,
or to the downward curve of your mouth
that indicates grief I have carried since birth.
Your nose I thought too wide, has lengthened with time
that forces decision, and your white thighs
that frightened me, console me through darkening nights.

What good shoulders you have, I admit;
your soft breasts amaze me, and curving mortal hips.
When I see you naked so, still scarcely known,
I wonder, have I not served you well enough,
neglecting, depriving you of proper lovers—
the surging, languorous caress of bluegreen ocean,
the wild and powerfully exacting dance.

What a different story had I lived for you,
my devoted, solid, healthy Body,
with your hands of a potter or a surgeon,
strong enough to gather grain for a life of simple
satisfying eating. What patience you have shown
this lethargic, sedentary, moody being
who borrowed you, she claims, for higher reason.

Sitting waiting, while she thinks and dreams,
craving only quiet spaces, beauty in which
to lose herself on ever longer, more voluptuous
and deeper journeys, you must be a saint.
With your delicate, hyper-sensitive nerves—
painstakingly cultivated by erratic Mother Karma
who one moment forgets, the next grips violently—

so aware everything irritates or gives you
overwhelming pleasure, ecstatic wicked Body,
maniacally driven from one unreachable extreme
to another, isn't it obvious how, torn
between joy and terror, you became a poet,
passionately vibrating instrument, house
of the certain yet doubting, ever shifting eye.

Earthbody, brief spouse, what a strangely
inconvenient marriage. Yet you are my only
true support. And though you may never
fathom what I secretly am, may you—
who accepted the nature of existence itself—
stay with me in your lovely halo of death
till I depart, dearest Body, my slave, my queen.

A Divine Meal

I am an old fashioned type
who likes a meal to pass slowly,
not one of those modern hygienic or ancient ascetic types
who likes a soiled plate whisked away.

Fast is best when buying tickets to the movies
but not when eating the Goddess' own body
or blood from her wildly radiant vine.
I'm no puritan at mealtime.

I like my disheveled plate with a well-licked fork
sprawling satisfied across it,
a pause between each dish
for emptying my mind and manifesting a new one.

Conversation too I like, voices harmonically arranged.
And food—the kind that tastes good.
I love my senses sublime, and a good cook
is one of the million gods I worship.

No, I'm not one of the obsessionally obese
driven by deadly numbing lust
to devour every perfection.
I am an old fashioned type—

one of the immortals, like you.
Service, for me, is a sacred word.
Every room is a temple, every table an altar.
And frankly, I find the food served here simply divine.

What I'm Worth

So,
sue me
for my coleus,
for my ten cats.
Sue me for my books
elegant
until the plumbing
flooded my basement in Lafayette.
Sue me for the air I breathe,
the food I eat,
the dreams I dream,
the sleep I sleep.
Sue me for my empty bed,
the clothes I wear,
my worn-out boots,
my many masks.
Sue me for the time I spend,
the time I'm late, the time I waste—
how about my secret thoughts,
my fears,
my angels and the miracles
I've witnessed.
The love, oh sue me for all
the love I've wanted,
all the love I've saved and craved,
the loved I've lied, the love I've denied,
the love I hid—don't forget the love
I've memory of, don't forget the things
I've learned, don't forget anything I'm telling you
or anything I forgot. There's no end to what
you can sue me for—sue me for my name!

When in France

When in France, put your elbows
on the table and order with heart, my dear.
Look at all the lovely lively people
chatting over a kir.

When in France, sink your fork
into leeks dripping heaven.
As the waiter gazes into your third eye,
savor the flavor and sigh.

When in France, indulge your beauty—
a small scarf, a silken vest,
some whirling gold earrings.
Your naked joie de vivre will suffice.

When in France, let your hair down,
bend eye to sparkling eye.
Let your feelings snap and soar
like a kite rising in the wind.

When in France, sing your desire
with your entire choir.
A mousse à l'amour
will send your coloratura even higher.

When in France, stay longer than you can.
Lay your fortune on the wheel,
and let this incarnation sweeten
like a fat pink carnation.

The Hunger

To hate, to love
requires a stone basement
where wines are stored
in spider-dark dampness—
a single light switch just by a door
that's strongly framed against earthquakes.
Then brick on brick and beam on beam,
all we think and all we feel press close
to hold the moment open
to light at night, and in the morning
more darkness.

*

Degrading myself, a cell
in communion with others,
I'm reduced to the pain that measures
the height I'll fill, fulfilling my purpose—
one foot sunk in unreason,
the other lifted forever onto the rock.
In this posture I greet you—a sculpture
carved by a former lover, mouth opened
on one unending syllable—intoxicated
with the words that rush through my vessels,
all carrying the one message: my life.

*

When you think
the last poem over,
does it scare you like a bare breast?
My hunger so blatant, my dream
a gourmet meal so easily distilled
to throbbing suck: chocolate-chip cookies and milk,
eggs Benedict served with champagne,
coquilles St. Jacques—all richness
reduced to butter then milk
then mother. You must be shocked
I want to eat you.

A Night in Rome

A beautiful young couple in white and black shirts,
at a white clothed table on the Piazza Navonna,
ask the waiter to take their picture.
Over creamy cannelloni they smile,
as countless forms of humanity
parade the cobblestone square.

From somewhere, a tenor sings.
A horse-drawn carriage clops by
to no apparent destination.
The suave waiter in a smooth white jacket
presses his large brown long-lashed eye
to the lens, and clicks.

The silvery woman at a nearby table
needs no photo to recall the vivid instant—
only yesterday—she too promenaded in magic.
The lamp of the sky is softly lit.
The lights of the piazza slowly come on.
The waiters are jovial, consoling.

They know how brief is this delightful scene.
Nor does the ancient city bother
to scour its darkening walls—
soon, soon, they too will be rubble.
And the poet taking notation—who knows
how she will be cast in the next play.

III. MOVING TOGETHER IN THIS CONVERSATION

Backwards

Two years ago
you were teaching French
and writing a fairytale,
living in a cottage in the hills
with two cats
and a porch of plants.

Now
your legs are your arms,
your arms are your legs,
your mouth is a hungry penis,
you're growing hair,
wondering if you should get
a sex change.

When you take a shower,
people say, *You're backwards,*
aren't you!
Then you step back
into one of your past lives.

What else
becomes of poets
these days?

Widow

Help me! her husband cries.
Then his heart stops.
Propped against her in the taxi
he doesn't speak, kiss, or lift
a finger to object.

The next day she goes out to pump water,
flailing her body up and down
until the entire weight of it aches;
at night under stars
gashes her leg against the rail.

The coffin,
mounded with layers of earth,
bright stalks of tropical flowers,
submits to raising
and lowering.

She wakes in the dark,
picks up a mystery,
notices the banana trees,
rhododendrons, blackberries, lilies
engulfing the hollow house.

Look at the light on that tree, she exclaims.
Her new lover taps a cold finger on her knee.
She tugs down her skirt,
concentrating on something—
like a rainbow—faraway.

The Light

Even the trees are nervous. The light stays too late. The city is rimmed by an orange glow that reaches up to the night. The moon, little boat, holds an onyx guest. Venus steps out of the sky. An airplane—or a rocket—glides between them. The house contains warmth till well after dark. Meals last the whole night—steamed vegetables, garlic effervescences, ices melting in amber. The poet steps to her typewriter. A white cat lies languorously across the table. Acacias have burst wide open, and lavender lips of wisteria curl over their hard bud cases. The harbor floods with light.

A Grave

A large white lady pads past me, grimacing because I have let a man in my room. A little redhead limps over to my door, reminiscing about the War—how the Russians raped all the women and stole her furniture. She wants me to stay all day and fill my oven with smoking briquettes. Is shocked when I cut off my long brown hair. On the window ledge, under portraits of Goethe and Schiller, I set my flowering heather. On the old oak desk, my unfinished translations. On the slim hard bed my burgundy spread. When the snow falls in December I wake up and pack my bags, buy the return ticket and leave the heather. Behind the door the tall one shuffles. The short one shudders—*Don't you know heather belongs on a grave.*

Asking

After you have left, I hear the flute
play six notes and stop.
In the glow of the candles
you did not smile, your shadow
cast with the coleus against the wall.
Your hair flamed.

You asked *How do I look?*
and laughed, rocking on your chair,
hands clasped about your knees.
By the nighttime window
your face stood still.
Somber you looked, unexplained.

Wanting

She is carefully stepping over the important communications like cracks in the sidewalk. Even in the fluorescent lights she is inscrutable. She cultivates it: jaw down, mouth lifeless, melancholy cheekbones, eyes all depth. She wants the medal of honor. Nothing has shocked her. *Nothing is more improbable than reality,* she says. Fantasy can't hold a candle to it, that tiny dark room, crammed full of repetitions. She is prepared. She prays, in case. Forgets all she can, keeping her eye firmly on the present. *How poised,* they say, *how brave.* She is a success at the piano recital, she gets straight A's—a few B's cautiously woven in to placate the authorities. She can be amusing at dinner, she can cook. A charming daughter. Earnest, determined. Someone who will do something with her life. Someone with a long list of demands on life. Who will demand more with every disappointment. Who on the last day will argue with God, *We want something better.* Someone who can't stop, can't stop wanting.

Wife Dreaming

From the tower
you survey the landscape—
far below, your little husband
with his girl-kite rising
toward you.

You reach out, your long arms
drawing her in.
Carefully you untie
the string, as paper turns
softly to flesh.

Her familiar eyes smile back.
Immediately your hands
entwine in sweetness.
Clouds pass, the world swirls.
Only the tower stands perfectly still.

Doom

No one's fated or doomed to love anyone.
The accidents happen...like car crashes.
—Adrienne Rich

After the crash, you sat plastered against the seat,
ranged like Garbo, like distance herself:
knitted cap and dark glasses, long angle of cheek,
mouth faint, evocative, lavender collar over
a slim run of torso, fine swinging lines of legs, a Kali hand.

What a hellish moment you articulated as I desired you
inappropriately, admiring your effective arrogance,
how you twisted me round your mind telling me
to back off—a strategy for divine comedians
who explore at leisure the backroads of soul.

I guess that's where I met you, crouched so I couldn't see
your face, meekly whispering, bare ankles disappearing
into your hiking shoes, slashed wrist turned over
in my palm for clinical evaluation: I held it a long time
as the car turned over and over and over.

Owl

Early on you learned
to bring design to the dark.
Hidden behind the door
you watched your father shoot and kill.
You grew without the rules.
Making unsolicited observations,
you made enemies as you saw through
arrogance, villainy, frozen hearts.

But Seer, could you see through
the weave you wove
to your death? I dreamed
you ran up the stairs to greet me,
sister seer—for I too must
bring to light memories
whose faces mock us like the stars.
We embraced, and then you

stepped off the staircase.
Let's extricate ourselves
and roll to safety, I whispered.
But you swallowed the pills
and sank in the steaming tub,
leaving a note composed
as a poem: *Lost—*
can't find the way back.

Standing on the other shore,
a stunted figure wobbles—
grim droopy cheeks, saggy shoulders,
rusty eyes returning to sand.
No enemies now—freely she
converses with Death.
In the night I see her owl eyes
and hear her hoo-hooting.

Icy Water

Two people jump off the Golden Gate for Christmas and Phyllis' manuscript arrives. Icy cold water. A woman in the water dragged ashore. Condition unknown. I am worried about Phyllis, her poems. They tell the truth. No jokes. No fire in the place. The poet is having a hard time. She is not in love and is trying to work out an old relationship. How long ago did it start? I ask. When you were just a girl playing with your red wagon? A large red bow tied around the wagon under the Christmas tree. An electric train from Santa Claus instead of brothers. The Christmas I was thirteen I snuck downstairs while everyone else slept. Alongside the tree, of equal stature, a golden harp. I swooned alone in love. I wanted to be an angel. When I plucked those strings I would be sweet. Pink organdy. Seated on your lap, swaddled in your perfume, your aura. Love. The woman jumped because of no love. Like a knife into icy water.

I Follow You

We are moving together in this conversation. You slipping into the hot black rubber suit—I am astonished but watch with my attention tuned to every detail. The waves are enormous and the water is cold. You go flapping down, your legs disappearing, your shoulders set in perfect balance with your partner's, then you go under. A great nebula of white foam follows this disappearing act, it seems to approach me faster than consciousness, I must be in the spacecraft soaring down the opaque midnight highway. Or you are saying, *Those waves are too wild, you go in if you want to, I'll stay up here and take some pictures.* In one a spray arcs up over a boulder—you arrested this moment with your fingers like a lace. The photographs lie spread on the table and we pore over them with incredible curiosity, but do not touch. Imperceptibly the bromeliad's green arm grows toward us. You step over to adjust the curtain and I follow you.

Evening Grace

The cat perches on the window sill
over banks of bright peach fog.
Debussy's melodies lilt on the radio.
A dog howls plaintively.
The cards show a death—midstream
the scorpion bit the camel it rode, and drowned.

In the violet light I take the chalice
and let the Graces dance.
A light breeze lifts the hair off my forehead,
stroking my face, dissolving the cruelties
I inflicted thinking I authored my fate.
The cat contemplates the orange and blue evening.

Sarangi Sorrow

Against the carnelian sky
a young man sits on the palace pool steps
and plays the sarangi his father once played.
Bow to string, he plays his soul.

Together we wander the white-walled labyrinth,
kneel on the dirt, drink sweet mint—
he can tell by the way I listen
some violent music has shattered my heart.

Oh nothing sobs like the sarangi—
it whines in the empty cavity,
it saws through grief until you worship grief
releasing its sundering song.

The young man's eyes are bright springs.
Each note climbs from the mud dripping gold.
Oh nothing surpasses the grandeur of sarangi sorrow—
sixteen thousand miles I voyaged to hear this sound

that drowns discarded love in raptured joy.
Oh nothing is sweeter than humiliation Sarangi plays.
Like jasmine, it rises from tinkling dust.
Beneath the towers in deepening desert dusk

a young man plays like his grandfathers.
For queens and strangers he plays until night
has drunk every tone. *Where are you,*
Sarangi cries, *among all these milky moping golden stars.*

Mysteries in the Garden

A little fat girl sits swinging and swinging.
From the house voices rise, strident and cruel.
Clouds glister on the water.
Everything shivers. Higher and higher
she swings into the silence.

*

An old man chops down
two rose trees twined over an arbor.
By the stump of the fire rose
he stacks logs to burn—or plant anew.
The woman waits for a cutting of the deeper red.

*

Scratching the dirt with burning fingers
she digs up the bones.
Give me what I need! she cries.
We can't, they mumble dissolving into dust,
disappointing her for the last time.

*

Two lilies float on the water.
No suffering, only the stillness of violet water.
Hope disappears in gauzy white petals.
Light enters yellow stamen.
Powdery pads float on the surface.

*

In one hand the scythe,
in the other hand the golden seed,
at Her feet a woman kneeling.
Flames rise. Charcoal petals
close over the past.

*

A woman buried herself in the garden.
Out of the poppies—roaring red, tender pink,
burnished green—she rises.
Mauve and blue trees enter her
as she spreads into the wide gold dusk.

A Cat Climbs

A cat climbs onto the downy bed,
stepping toward the magnificent woman
who stretches out her hand.
Like a cup she tilts her rosy palm
and pours herself into the tiny furry body
arching hungrily to drink.

Soon the cat is humming like a cello.
But already the woman is tired
of the fragile electric yearning
flooding the room with thrilling music.
With one grand sweep she empties the dregs
and sends the cat flying.

IV. ELEMENTS OF LOVE

Where You Are

Brown-eyed side
of darkness
angled cheek
of dream

I forgot
your lips that
flowered lushly

remember those
wide red roses that
laughed

at my desire

and then your neck
descended
to darkness

the rest of
imagination

a space

where no one
spoke

I wonder
these days where
you are

where
you are

The Treasure Box

Your nightmares will always be safe
in my treasure box painted
with crimson blossoms, enchanting birds.

Your nightmares belong with your jewels—
carnelian dreams, melting amber,
lazuli skies teeming with golden stars.

There whenever a child cries,
rivers rush turquoise, hearts pour ruby,
mirrors reflect only the night's beauty.

Starlings

I let go, but this love
won't leave me—
it circles and returns
like a flock of starlings.

Which way does the sky go,
and how will I get over
the barrier of your body
rolling green to the boundless horizon?

Oh, how the starlings in majestic formation
euphoric soar over rising mounds,
where layer on layer
civilizations lie down in star dust.

But starlings never forget—
like a deck of magic cards shuffling
they fall and reunite, scattering
the tall calm sky with their glitter.

The Elements of Love

The house is locked,
but I am the earth
and truer than fear.

The house is cold,
but I am the air
and truer than remorse.

The house is burning,
but I am the water
and truer than fury.

The house is gone,
but I am the fire
and truer than grief.

Reflect

Reflect on the dark
where fear is lost.

Reflect on the dark
where light begins.

Reflect on the dark
where gold is dancing.

Death, Great Friend (V–VII)

This loss goes on and on. You're never coming back, and no one can replace you. I think of your epic dreams, in which the history of the twentieth century unfolded. What was in the air was as concrete to you as to me—intuitions exchanged without obstacle. You saw evil, were eager to fight for good. You hounded me when I strayed in loneliness.

Pretty, dark-eyed, your shining olive-rose skin blended with the landscapes of Galilee. Your warm voice sharpened when something was wrong; what you liked made you laugh like a baby. Happiness, righteousness, clarity you invented as you danced and drew. And then your ovaries, that made three glory eggs, revolted, generating meaningless cells, chaos, death. How this loss goes on and on. You're never coming back. And no one can replace you.

*

You're nothing but a crushed flower now, soft and frail—like the petaled velvety vulva you painted with my face looking out. Oh, those female faces we wore, looking on with horror. There's no hope for changing the world—giant organism chaotic, cruel, crushing in its cornucopious productions, moments of perfect inspiration followed by inevitable deflation.

Attachment brings pain, non-attachment the void, doing freely for others both joy and violent punishment. *Now you see what the world is like,* said Tolstoi. Non-world bathes psyche and nature like sunlight or silver mist in these portraits of life—ungraspable souls hinted on paper and canvas: our lone lives.

*

Children flown to Los Angeles, New York; husband remarried; pictures gone from the walls; the house sold—no sign left of you. Only your voice, my Soul, keeps calling. You're permanent now, Friend who'll always be near me. You haven't changed a bit. Oh Death, Great Friend, what huge arms You have, vast enveloping wings. You spread them and we fly, dark and shining blue into the sun.

Rubies

Rubies, it's not your fault
you were given in passion.

Rubies, it's not your fault
you were pried from your bed.

Rubies, it's not your fault
you were crystallized with lies.

Rubies, it's not your fault
you were bloodied by love.

Rubies, it's not your fault....

Meeting My Fate

My white dog pulled me to the door. I knocked, and it opened. A magnificent woman rose off her chair, greeting me in a voice that pealed like an old mission bell. I shrank back and pulled my dog with me. I hadn't even bothered to change my clothes—still had on my jeans, and a white tee shirt painted with pink and turquoise symbols. It was a hot afternoon.

Along the wall I slunk toward a table where our hostess had set out the drinks. Pouring myself a tall tonic, I glanced around the room. The only empty seat was a small chair nestled against the body of the large woman, who I now saw wore black.

I sipped my drink slowly, thinking. There was no other place to sit. Resolutely I stepped toward the uncomfortable stool and squatted down, leaning as far forward as possible, keeping my eyes lowered to the carpet so I could not see her.

But she had already resumed her commanding tone. I can stop this, I thought, ejaculating syllables sharp and cold as ice cubes. As the last sound melted in the air, something snared my attention, and I lifted my head slightly. On her broad breast lay sleeping birds of turquoise, mother-of-pearl and shining onyx.

How beautiful! I gasped with uncontrollable passion, raising my face all the way up to her luminous smile. Her eyes were beaming. One was an exquisite sapphire that reflected the wide blue sky. The other contained a broken iris that sprawled into darkness.

The Joy

Along the hills of your body
I rooted in the fragrant earth.

Stretching my blossoming arms
I heaved with offerings.

I was a peach dripping gold
and you drank me.

I was a cry in the forest
that pierced your windy heart.

I was a comet tumbling
across your moonlit valley.

I was a woolly lamb in your pen
who was stripped by the shearing night.

Listen! In the bleeding womb of life
there are rhythms that can never be broken.

Tumbling Back to Earth

I remember that journey back into the body,
down corridors occupied by phantoms,
tubes in every orifice rushing air and water
to save your life.

I remember that writhing to be free
as you twist against restraints, and groaning fail;
for once I too could not bear life's pain,
gulped every pill and nearly died.

And I remember that great surge of Life after,
reclaiming me in its dharmic service.
Squirming and grimacing, you still don't understand—
Why am I here? you ask.

Soon you'll remember—first the guilt,
then the laughter. Turning over,
you resemble one of Rubens' rosy angels
tumbling back to Earth—and I embrace you.

The Lover

Your skin was midnight satin.
And I was a brilliant seeker.

Your heart was mother of pearl.
And I was a baby oyster.

Your voice was doting honey.
And I was parched for sweetness.

Your eyes divined other worlds.
And I was a starry stranger.

Your mind was a windblown encyclopedia.
And I was a fanatic scholar.

Your words were silken knots.
And I was a master of paradox.

Your lotus opened a thousand petals.
And I was a bee—I dove to your center.

Two Pears

We were two pears hanging on a tree.
You were gold, and I still green.
I thought we would always be together.
One day a violent wind took you instantly.

You plunged to the loamy world below.
While I, left hanging, growing juicier,
was soon devoured by a throng of raucous birds
whose bittersweet song you now hear.

Heartbreak

How could you, stone by stone, tear down our house
where rooms flared from the spiraling center
and doves cooed in the dreaming sun.

How could you contemptuously turn
and rage down the aspiring tower
that gazed beyond bridges into every direction.

How could you abandon those spaces young and yearning,
gutting our cupboard, bed and hearth,
while the sun gilded the West with sacred fire.

How could you storm past hummingbirds sipping
at fuchsia altars and flee the guardian pines at the gate,
just as I shattered and our love was born.

Karmic Forest

It wasn't our fault—the Gods sundered us.
We were two tall trees that grew together,
bark in bark, our inner rings locked.

Was it Kali wielded the ax that seared our bodies
crimson and sliced our woven roots, riding out
of Durga's forehead, her tongue beheading the world?

We teetered and swayed, must have fainted,
crashing into the silence; now our torn roots
that reveled in thirst are stone coils seeking nothing.

So let the little children climb up
on our throne-like trunks, that will lie rotting
in the glistening wet for eons to come.

And our scaly green fronds that drank the light
and filled the forest with breath—
let the crows pluck these rusty wands for their nests.

No, it was not our fault—fate demanded this death.
Every scene was perfectly staged, and we,
let it forever be said, were magnificent falling.

My Grief

Queen, my
broken tall grass,
I never knew
that you were mine.

My Heart

My heart is pouring itself out of me.
My heart is soaring toward you over thousands of miles.
My heart comes nearer and nearer.
My heart longs to enter...

Like ten fingers running over the keys,
like a powerful stream that has ever been flowing,
like a flock of night birds lit by the moon—
I am flying after my heart.....

What Remains

Here, you forgot something—
it's your love.
I found it after you left.

V. THE SOUND OF CHANGE

Last Words

Justine's father sat in a wheelchair, his emphysema far advanced. He was panting arduously, as if trudging up the last steep mountain in a lifetime of hard work. After so many years of painful breathing, ineffable joy suddenly lifted him up. Happily he greeted his long lost friends. "That's different from anything I've ever heard of," he thundered with amazement. And then, with cosmic dismay, "What a crazy price." Those were his last words.

Justine's younger sister tried spooning him some soup—but that only triggered the final coma. Her father's commanding head fell over. They had to carry him to bed. Justine automatically stepped back, so the other members could say their good-byes. As she stood in the corner of the room next to the stuffed green parakeet she had recently given him, she could feel her father, like her, watching—he had already left his body—this final scene.

He had been home from school, sick, the day his father's model A Ford skidded fatally over ice into a giant sycamore. After the farm was sold, his family headed to California, where he and his brother found work picking oranges. He knew he would never go to college—he would have to learn from the books of Experience. After he met the stunning dark-eyed Maria, he bought an orange grove with thousands of orange trees, and Justine was born. He had been a tender father. But most of the time he was at work. His whole life he had been at work.

The sun was setting over the magnificent blue Pacific, leaving an intense orange sky. The silvery old man lay back, gasping on his bed. His wife knelt on one side of the bed, and Justine's sister knelt on the other. Another sister was missing—abdicated long ago. Justine gazed softly at the lean, well-used body, sucking over wet gravel its last lingering breath. "Dearest, we'll join you," her mother cried. "Soon," her sister added, strangely emphatic.

Late that night—about two o'clock—Justine woke up and went to her father's room. Someone had closed his mouth. He looked like a marble sculpture, deeply carved by life. An authoritative hawk's beak guarded the mouth. Justine sat for a long time in the dim silence. And then she was three, standing on the sidewalk, her little arm raised, hand tightly clasped in her father's wide freckled hand. He looked both ways for any oncoming cars, as the wind blew through his thick black wavy hair, and through the waving fronds of the palm trees.

Justine saw her father for the last time only a few nights later in a dream. She stood at her window, gazing out. High above in another building, her old father climbed into bed. She waved as hard as she could—but he never saw her.

A Good Laugh

Justine knocked several times on Plum's door. When he didn't answer, she carefully opened it and stepped inside. "Plum, are you here?" she called. "Upstairs, Dear. Come on up." She took the stairs two at a time and strode into the bedroom.

Plum sat on the bed, surrounded by collapsing piles of books. "Now you know why an old man needs a queen-sized bed," he chuckled with a twinkle in his eye. Justine sat down on the edge of the bed, and Plum took her hand in his, squeezing it. "To be honest, I prefer these dear friends to the poverty people around me call relationships—doings based primarily on convenience, finance, vanity and lust. Arrangements in which each person is scarcely aware of the real existence of the other. And these," now his voice turned tender. "What are they—?" His trembling old hand swept over his books, as if conducting an orchestra. "These little boxes contain vast worlds. They are the outer manifestation of inner lives."

Justine got up and paced around the room, glancing at the thousands of volumes that filled the surrounding shelves. Beautiful artifacts from Plum's travels—statues, clay pots, weavings—were wedged inbetween them. "No, I never became a writer. Never had the time. Too busy thinking. I could spend ten lifetimes thinking, there is so much to think about. And sometimes lately, I think I'm beginning to have my first real thought. When I finally get my thoughts, I'll be able to begin my philosophy."

Justine settled down into the worn leather chair across from Plum. "What do you think life is all about, really, Plum?" Her tone was serious now. "Why are we here?"

"According to my books," he answered without a pause, "there are three theories. Love, Power, and Work. The Love people say the universe has a heart, and all of creation is nothing but a sublime goodness machine invented by God—for our own good. The Power people, on the other hand, believe the universe is founded on supreme Malevolence, an emptiness at the core of creation which man must resist falling into—with every dyne of his minuscule force.

Whereas the Work Theory proclaims that human beings actually make a difference in the final outcome of Creation, depending on their choice of good or evil. This is where morality comes in—a word, incidentally, I positively dread, for it has been used as a synonym for hate more than any other word I know. That's why I say, just give me my beloved books, my thoughts, my dreams, my observations, and my endless ruminations. But *please* keep that obscene word out of it."

Justine's attention was riveted. "And which theory do you believe in, Plum?" she asked with passionate urgency rising in her voice. Plum leaned back slowly until he touched the wall. Suddenly he looked hundreds of years old. Something like a tear was pressing itself out of the corner of one dim blue eye. He had little hair left, and what there was of it was white as a ghost's. He clasped his wrinkled hands together. "Naturally, I'd *like* to believe in the Love Theory—like all those fortunate saints who see nothing but Love everywhere—in every frown, under every rock—as if the whole cosmos were nothing but a giant gorgeous flower pulsating with triumphant joy. —And I'm working on it.

Meanwhile—until Grace reveals Herself to me naked, until She comes and tells me personally that God really is Love—I'll believe in the Work Theory. It gives me sufficient hope, and seems to agree with both my optimistic nature, and all of the suffering I've been through and seen with my own eyes.

Ah, let us not even speak of those demons who say that existence is nothing but an empty power game, in which the petals of the cosmos are made of plastic, and even the skin of the Gods is fake.

My dear little Justine, the universe is most certainly a circus. It has a ring for love, a ring for power, and a ring for work. And I wonder how many other rings there may be as well. The universe is like one of those busy, yet harmonious Tibetan paintings. Agnostics, like ostriches, hang around the periphery, burying their heads in the sand. And just beyond them I see the tormented crazies, buried up to their heads, mouths producing a cacophony of petty resentments.

You see, the older I get, and the weaker my eyes become, the more I can see. Oh, It has curves, all right. It has the power of an eternal thunderbolt. It is happening. Beauty is created constantly everywhere. And love—I am sure of it—is yet to come. There are ideas, like the idea of love, that connect us. And mystic streams that heal us. And there is never-ending harm. The whole is a splendid vast writhing joyous and suffering Serpent, shedding Her skin as She wiggles along, perpetually revealing a new Self that rises from Her own pure delight.

Ah, Justine, It is luminous, explosive, awesome and miraculously funny! Do you get the incredible joke? Can you hear the roaring gusto of Her laughter? There really is nothing but this sound, my child. Awful, perhaps, but listen closely!" Now Plum stood, and moving toward her, fell down at her feet. "Can you hear all of Her voices—each different, and all of them laughing. In that laughter is everything. And it is so important to laugh along, and never stop laughing. There simply isn't time for anything else. So take my hand, dear, and join me in a good laugh—it will add a little spice to the side-splitting symphony of laughter. Oh, let the tears of laughter roll shamelessly down your cheek, as her skins keep falling away. For laughter is the very sound of change.

—Now there's a thought."

Into the Vineyard

The white puppy hopped into the back seat. The older samoyed waited for Justine to lift her hind legs and boost her in. Then Justine climbed into the car and backed it out of the driveway. The light was already fading as she accelerated toward the plaza. At the corner her eye gravitated toward a woman in magenta tights, dancing in the street to the thumping rock band that blared from the historic stone hall. Gigantic clusters of burgundy balloons rose up into the evening sky over the townspeople seated on the grass, sipping their supper wine. The bear flag of the renegade Republic of California flapped softly in the breeze.

Ah, the carnival of life, Justine sighed inwardly, as her car purred on, full of its own purpose. Turning left on Fourth Street, it headed toward the hills and took another left onto Ravenswood. The narrowing road curved through a dense bower of large bay trees that overwhelmed her with their powerful cleansing scent. Beyond them rose the terraces. She pulled up sharply under an old scrub oak.

The sun was already behind the hills. Justine and the dogs made their way quickly past the dark red roses—bending over, she kissed their perfumy lips—onto a rocky road that had been plowed through the valley. Row after row of lush leafy twisting vines with small green grapes passed them, as the woman and her dogs mounted the beautifully terraced hills. For a moment Justine stopped, looking upward. The rim of the hills glowed a soft deep blue, back-lit by the invisible sun. Over them hovered a white sickle, cupping a black velvet ball. Beyond, Venus twinkled merrily. And beyond Her—the vastly scattered stars. Music drifted down from somewhere—likely one of the remote homes wedged into the darkening hillside.

The air was cooling off. Justine wore a cotton sweater that still made her feel too warm. Careful in the dimming light, she stepped over the rocky deep-red earth. The wolf-dogs followed, the younger racing joyfully ahead and returning anxiously, uncertain of Justine's direction; the older arthritic dog wobbling forward with experienced enthusiasm. Beyond the vines, the rolling hills were cloaked in gnarled live oaks, that were rapidly transforming into black masses. Her gaze rested on a mysterious single light atop the highest hill.

In the growing dark Justine walked on, unable to see, yet one with the earthy road, thickly caked with the Mother's blood. As she moved she became the blood, all the blood that had ever flowed, and that was flowing inside her full-bodied now. Entering the hills, she rose into a golden green light that merged into the sun, the fire of Creation, the ultimate energy, the shakti. Then she fell, slowly, back into the moonlit night where a million stars shimmied, everything radiant with its own fire, everything basking in epiphany.

She felt her own glow warming the night, as she walked on.

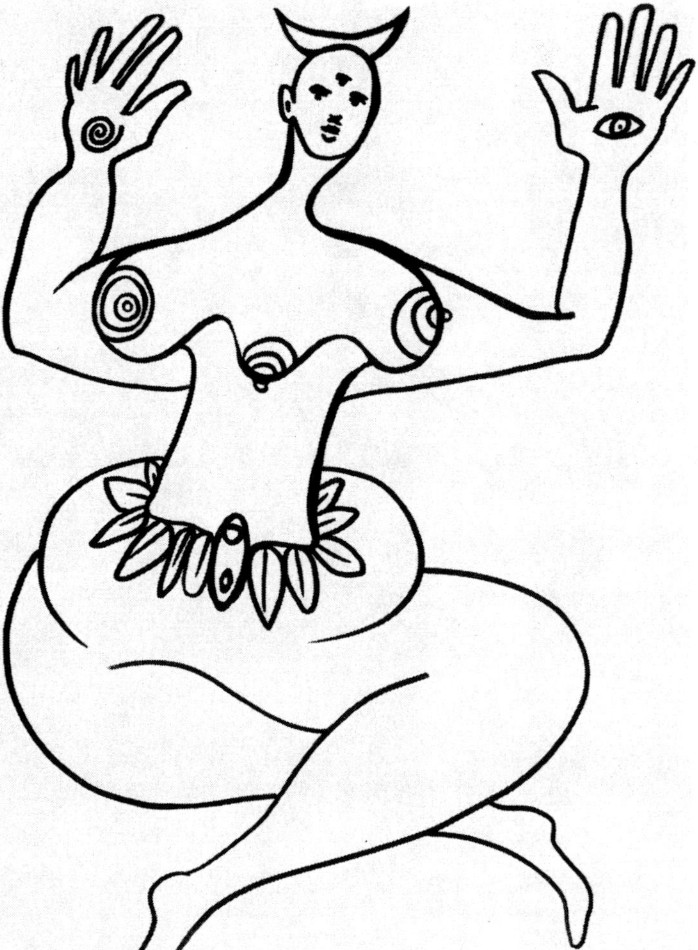

VI. NATURAL TRAVELERS

Kate's Song

To Kate Wolf

She was the singer who sang her heart:
You must give yourself to love,
if love is what you're after.

Guitar in her arms, she sang her heart:
There's a wind blowing down the canyon,
so hot and dry the rocks turn red.

Through tears and laughter, she sang her heart:
Grandmother Earth, give me a rest,
I take my place with the Woman in the West.

Plutonium in her bones, she sang her heart to death.

Mother's Child

Aija, in that little south German town, early Sixties, studying in the basement apartment, stone, with a lookout through the Black Forest, where one night you sat alone and watched the storm from start to finish, trees drenched, a drowned marsh at your feet, then—though no one would believe it later—a spectacular show of pink yes pink lightning, a lace like your grandmother would have woven decades back in Latvia—you beside her sipping warm milk and honey—though Latvia barely existed, a Russian land-patch with German soldiers retreating, where you were born, carried in your grandmother's arms to the refugee camp in Berlin, from which you fled, all six of you, to Petaluma and chicken farms—where your grandmother died and you, fourteen, became your mother's child.

Singing

To Denise Levertov

White-winged poet
though angel of peacock feathers
and scarlet spiny flames in your poem
you minister to the wounded still
volume after volume to the damaged
and hidden strangers who lift your wings
to read their compassionate secrets
power? facing the horrible deeds
of the dying race and reporting
the details to the living
but in your dream
your wings large luminous lift
over the cities the hospitals the war
and the angel of white soars
singing

Whatever You Want

Catherine Jackson is seated at the harp. With frizzy gray hair, dangling earrings and long powdered nose. Long bare arms, gathered satiny skirt with hand-painted flowers spread over her knees. *My mother said I'd never amount to a hill of beans.* Her strong callused fingers press into the strings. Then swishing out the door, her high laugh a glissando, she lifts her foot—in its elevated red leather shoe—into her yellow jeep and disappears over the hill. Her handwriting swirls gaily over the page: *You can do whatever you want.*

A, R, T

To Carolyn Kizer

As I read your poems sipping champagne,
the faucet chimes in a porcelain cup.
I look up from my couch—light glows on the hills,
a breeze shakes the pines, and sparrows sing.

A real poet, I say, and start for the typewriter,
heart lifting toward that altar.
But dull dread engulfs me and I sink in my sandy flesh,
spirit plunging back into its dark nest.

But you, at three, chose the blocks A, R, T,
(though now you mock your mother's proud tale).
You make the poems few can hear, solemnly
spoken over the void—solitude to solitude.

Vermilion Flower

Emily Dickinson is staying at home. She's wearing her white eyelet dress, wandering in her night garden, composing a poem. Her father sleeps. Emily Dickinson writes a letter to Mr. Higginson. *Is it any good, Sir?* she laughs. She's been growing many years now, pulling up weeds from China, sighting a lark over France, stunned by the evening sun in her backyard as Amherst turns past—the opal herd, the amber farm. Emily Dickinson has a solemn face. Her eyes are very strange. They're dark and look inward and out. Stars sparkle in the back of her head. In her hand—the vermilion flower outstretched.

Gloria

Anatomist? Two hundred years ago
they would have burned her at the stake—
she's a witch!

Gloria's mother came home late every night
from the dress factory, carping at her girls.
Gloria's black eyes harden.

Have you seen the way she handles the cadavers—
it's very sexual. Imagine, each morning she gets up,
puts on her blond wig, makeup, and comes to the lab to dissect.

Gloria's hair is black as shiny fur.
She leans forward, mother of two daughters,
medical student at thirty-four.

When some kid in class asked why she uses plaster models instead
of cadavers, she answered, "Do we have the right to use cadavers at all,
unless we too give our bodies to be dissected after we are dead?"

And Gloria, whose Italian grandmother
scoured floors till you could eat off them,
smiles triumphant, striding life and death.

Sappho of Eressos

Sappho looks up, angry about the myths—*small and dark with unshapely wings*—that wish to enclose her name. Still she laughs, glowing like the evening. A pink and orange smile crosses the sky. She touches her wrinkles—warm like the sand, like the hillsides of Lesbos, where bright oleander gush from the gullies, fingers of lavender and fragrant thyme. She touches those dry roads, and sees herself strolling in a dusty dream—seven-string lyre hanging at her side, dress twined like the olive tree whose upper arms are jubilantly silver. Or weaving lithe as summer grass in the open square, song rising like a nightingale from the droning plane tree, where children scream and old men grimace.

Suddenly a terror grips her—*Am I that woman running after Phaon, tiny man, flinging herself from White Cliff into Aegea's sparkling blue arms? Am I the midget statue with only one wing, the one whose face is broken off, or the oiled white Romantic marble?*

In truth, she is a strong swimmer who dives and frolics like a dolphin, large head shining at the surface, shadow dodged by schools of flickering fish. Rules have not harmed her expressive festive face. Her voice, rich and resonant, knows every stone and hollow of the scale. She is a natural traveler, loves the warm air of the islands, smelly with vegetables and flowers. But she is banished from her home. The Church burns her manuscripts in Constantinople, would have burned her at the stake but she escapes. Mummies sleep in the rags of her poems. The red hydria, decorated with her fine dreaming face, stands empty.

She married, they say, was wealthy and bore a daughter. But she scarcely remembers. They say she was a priestess *pure and holy.* She remembers sitting in the temple dark and listening. When the girls rush in like winds with their urgent wishes, she bows and adores. They say she worshipped Aphrodite. Indeed there is one brown arm warm and trembling, that pleases her as no other. Over it she runs her lips night after night, to learn forever its exquisite familiar shape—words, certain syllables, burning so powerfully in her mind no others can approach them. Alone she descends the earth's deep lips, her bare foot gleaming. At dawn her heart is flooded with song.

Sappho lowers her head, pale behind the slate-blue mountains. Gulls glide into the harbor, where her voice is lapping at the shore. Along the promenade couples preen and babble in a different Greek. In the courtyard two peacocks sigh in stone. Under hills of crushed pottery, mosaics in the sand, groan the streets and libraries of ancient Eressos. Near the horizon fish fly into the sea.

Samson

When I cut your hair off, it fell—
beautiful golden locks—away,
and for the first time I saw your face.
You looked fine without all that power.

I saw a gentleness I had never seen before.
Your mouth was sweet, your voice amber embers.
You warmed me with your words,
those coal like dreams through a long night.

Several times the sun rose and set again.
We were radiant, two lions, two laughing gods.
Your spirit felt like rain and mine like the desert.
In Canaan, in some future or formerly, we must have been one.

Akhmatova

Akhmatova, the oriole is always grieving—
is she happy or sad?
Silver willow sliced to a stump.

Suddenly she came out of that trance
and whispered in my ear (everyone spoke in whispers there),
"Can you describe this?"

Lyre that became a rattle —
you burned your poems and bellowed
a shroud over Stalingrad.

And I said, "Yes, I can."
Then something like the shadow of a smile
crossed what had once been her face.

Today in Petersburg the melting snow
drips off your bronze eyelids.
And the stars above—are they happy or sad?

The Passion Of Georgia O'Keeffe

How bright the light! Baby sits on pillows,
white and black quilt with flowers and stars.
Dust sparkles warm and soft—I want to eat it
but Mama snatches and squeezes me hard.

I'm going to be an artist, make something beautiful
as the Maid of Athens in Mama's book
or the Arabs on horseback in Grandmother's parlor.
An artist can do as she pleases, no one minds.

Have drawn a man tumbling over, am painting
a lighthouse in clouds. Sister with big eyes
doesn't like my small dark drawing of hands.
Must paint larger and lighter—purple lilacs, yellow corn.

Am disgusted with my work, and am glad.
Must forget everything learned, find the shapes
that are mine. I am the prairie thirsting.
I am the sky changing. I am the wind stirring.

My room is bare and white like a mirror.
In black, hair back, I walk toward the blazing horizon;
scorched, chilled, dust-caked, make my way
down gypsum trail through the mud canyon.

New York! At my easel on the highest story
I gaze upon roofs, trees, cliffs, clouds,
barges, bridges, smokestacks, soot plumes, steel beams,
skyscraper crowned with chromium needle.

For hours I bathe in the light as Stieglitz photographs
my hair, eyes, torso, long-fingered hands.
Fold on fold, clean pink, yellow, blue,
from my glass palette I paint the shapes in my mind.

Hipbone, labium, petal, leaf. In the deep green
veins arch apart; a lake settles in the center.
Lily, orchid, iris, rose, magnolia,
Jack-in-the-pulpit, poppy, petunia, trumpetflower.

Oh the sun! Sweet-smelling desert sage.
After stupor of sadness, sand dunes, mesas,
wide blue space. How my heart races.
Eyes sharpen and soften, skull a flower of bone.

Seven a.m., cool morning, car under cliff,
I turn the car seat and paint. Brown, orange, violet, gray.
Peach slopes cook to red. Clouds boil up black
and thunderous, trampling the slopes to wine.

Climbing the ladder onto the roof—
how big the moon, and soft. Pale silver crawls
over black. Above, the vast dome of stars.
Asleep, I feel the tender fingers of first morning light.

Over my wonderful world the pink and blue dawn
spreads to the snow-capped peak
of Sangre de Cristo, faraway and serene.
Purple asters waken on the shimmering plain.

White Place, hills of ancient lava ash,
turreted and spired with gray and red.
Black Place, pink and gold-veined, rollicking elephants
where sea once pounded and dinosaurs fed.

That's my mountain—Blue Pedernal
where Changing Woman was born. God told me
I could have it, if I painted it enough.
Never good enough, my failures lead me on.

Maria loads on logs, food, water, canvas, the cat.
Car inches along the dry riverbed.
I shovel sand, chop sage, roll away rocks,
paint with my gloves on in the wind.

At forty-five I take what I want—
Ghost Ranch on golden plain. Purple hills,
rotting cedar, light that illumines death.
The world is always at war, atomic lab just miles away.

Empty pelvis. Pelvis bursting with sun.
Winged pelvis with moon. Antler, jaw, sacrum—
the immortal body. Shadows lengthen, colors fade,
I paint alone until dark. I chose my fate.

Stieglitz is gone. Friends go too. Red hills
whiten with snow. Nearer and farther
a large black crow flies over the slope
into clear cold night.

I know what I must paint now—I paint
what I love. Instinct directs me.
Flowers, stones, bones instruct me.
Details are confusing—I observe, select, eliminate.

Ruthlessly I search for meaning inside things.
Tearing roots from my heart,
arrange in ever broadening light icons, offerings,
blessings that come from, return to life.

That door leads to my paintings. It's a curse
the way I keep painting it—green, red, from the side,
through the window, in shadow, with clouds, steps,
snowflakes, leaf drifting by. Now my last door.

Sleeping in the patio on my white bed
I gaze out over Green Valley.
Rocks and horns rest on the wall, patted pink
adobe skin soft against the dusty sky.

Have I gone mad with love? Everything
in my house lives! Listen, they call me
white-haired sorceress. In long black skirt
I stroll with my stick and ferocious chows.

My housekeeper tells me the names
of the colors and passing clouds.
My vision is blurred. My wrinkle-hooded
turquoise eye sees. I work—what else is there?

Sitting still in the sun I'm happy.
The sky is my companion. My spirit moves
in this light. Soon my ashes will sleep in these hills,
while the wind trills on about nothing.

Girls among the Ruins

Tonight in Teatro Marcello
two young Romans in long black dress
play flute and piano.
Past massive stones of the ancient apartments
the boulevard traffic courses.
A few capped columns stand at attention
as fluid sonatas permeate
the warm filthy air.
No longer required to serve tyrants,
the stones relievedly crumble
as the girls gaily trill on.

Long brown hair cascades down one slim back,
a dark crop crowns the other,
as four bare arms
move among moonless ruins.
In glaring spotlights
the audience listens, speechless.
Cars grumble louder and louder, but the flute
does not allow them to drown her out.
Leaning into the notes, she intones
deeper, charging the night
with her radiant will.

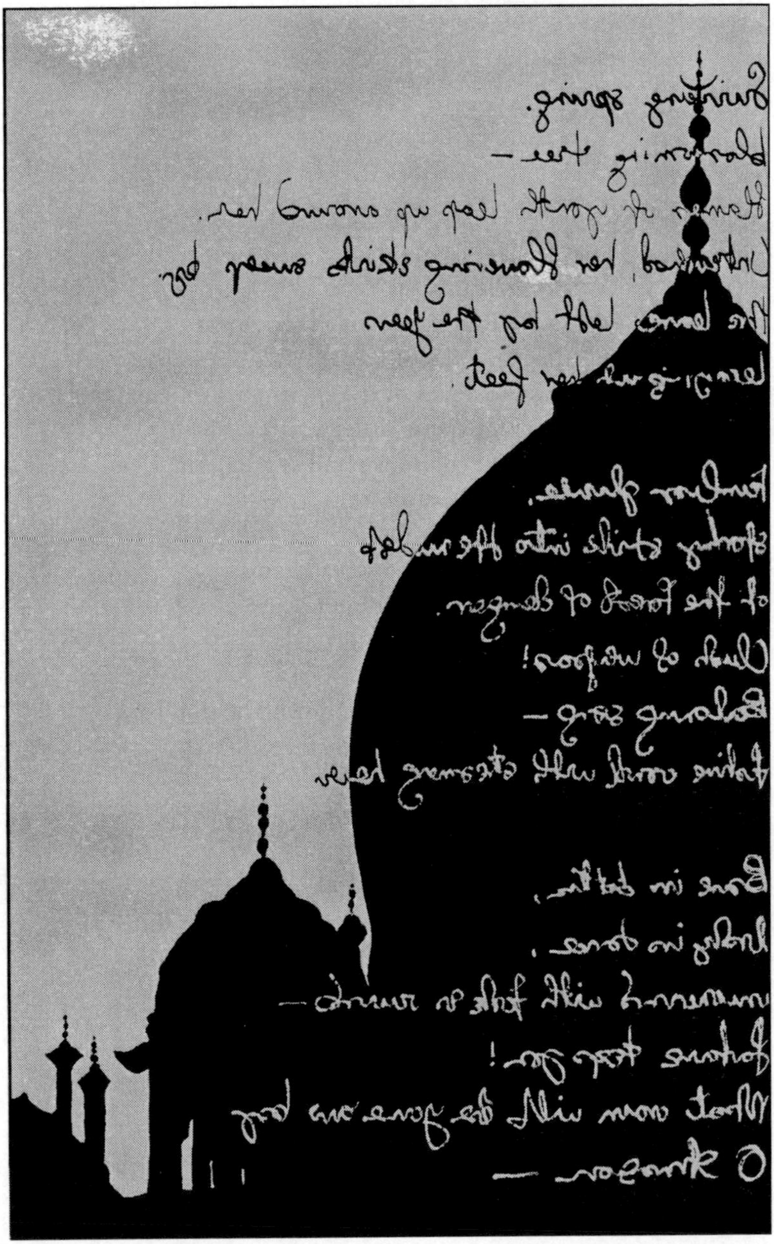

VII. IN OTHER WORDS (TRANSLATIONS)

Erotic
by Marguerite Yourcenar

You the wasp and I the rose,
you the spume and I the rock;
in the strange metamorphosis
you the phoenix and I the pyre.

You Narcissus and I the spring,
my eyes reflecting your emotion;
you the treasure and I the coffer;
I the tide, the swimmer inside me.

And you—mouth upon mouth—
the languor lulling the fever,
the billow dissolving in waves.

Whatever the tender game,
the soul on fire always flying away—
exquisite gold bird into the wide blue sky.

Your Name
by Marguerite Yourcenar

Your name given to you by your mother.
Your name poured down my bitter throat like a drop of poison honey.
Your name I cried under every sky and wept in every bed.
Your name I read in the water-marks on every page of my misery.
Your name clear as a tear shed on us by one of the Angels.
Your name like a beautiful naked child who rolled in the mud.
Your name that bruises my mouth.
Your name I sleep with like a talisman.
Your name like a sentence condemning me to banishment.
Your name I moan like a beggar who keeps lamenting
even at the gates of a city in flames.
Your name on which so many sordid stories perch like flies.
Your name people speak as if it were just anyone's.
Your name X for the unknown that is your self.
Your baptismal name inscribed in the black register of the Devil
and the golden book of God.
Your name nothing could ever make me forget.
Your name, with your memory the only thing you can never
take from me, since anyone under blue heaven may utter it.
Your name, whose every letter is a nail in my crucifixion.
Your name, the only one I'll remember on resurrection morning.

Love

by Mirabai

Do not mention the word love,
my naive companion.
The path turns strange
once you offer your love.
Your body is crushed at the first step.
If you want to offer love,
be prepared to cut off your head
and sit on it;
to circle the lamp like a moth
and drop your body;
to present your head like a deer
hearing the hunter's horn;
to swallow burning coals like a partridge
in love with the moon;
to yield your life like a fish
parted from the ocean;
to surrender like a bee
trapped under closing lotus petals.

Mira's Beloved lifted a mountain
with one little finger.
She says, Offer your mind to Those lotus feet.

O Mind, Worship
by Mirabai

O Mind, worship the lotus feet
that cannot be destroyed.
Between heaven and earth everything passes away.
Why fast or make pilgrimages?
Why bother with abstract talk?
Why attempt suicide under the blades of Benares?
Life is but the play of sparrows—
it ends with the arrival of night.
Why don an ochre robe and go wandering?
Whatever you wear, if you do not enter the Source,
you will be caught in the net of return.

Mira loves Krishna.
She cries, Sever every knot in my heart!

An Old Tibetan Carpet
by Else Lasker-Schüler

Your soul in love with mine
is woven with it in the Tibetan carpet.

Beam in beam, enamored colors,
stars that wooed across the heavens.

Our feet rest upon the treasure
thousands upon thousands of meshes wide.

Sweet lama son on a musk-plant throne,
how long has your mouth kissed mine.
And cheek upon cheek, how many lifetimes brightly tied.

Song of the Blessed
by Else Lasker-Schüler

Sabaoth speaks out of the evening:
Be prodigal, spend all your love!
So I may give you my crown pearls,
transform your blood into golden drops of honey
and soak your lips with the scent of sweet almonds.

Be prodigal, spend all your love!
And gild my feasts with molten jubilation,
planting in the melancholy that weighs on Jerusalem
singing umbrella blossoms.

And your heart will become a splendid garden
where the poets dream.
Oh your heart will become a hanging garden,
homeland of every dawn.
And stars will enter your nights
whispering their light.
Yes, your arms will raise a thousand reaching branches—
rocking, soothing my passion to return to paradise!

Night Secret
by Else Lasker-Schüler

I have chosen you
among all these stars.

Am awake, a listening flower
in the buzzing bush.

Our lips long to make honey,
our shimmering nights are in full bloom.

From your body's holy spark
my heart lights its heavens.

All my dreams hang from your gold.
I have chosen you among all these stars.

Homesick
by Else Lasker-Schüler

I cannot speak the language
of this cool country
or keep its pace.

Even the fleeting clouds
I cannot interpret.

Night is a step-queen.

Forever I must remember Pharoah's forests
and kiss the image of my stars.

My lips sparkle brightly
telling of faraway.

I am a colorful picture book
lying open on your lap.

But your face spins
a veil of weeping.

The corals were gouged
from my glittering birds.

Upon the garden bushes
their soft nests turned to stone.

Who will consecrate my dead palaces?
They held the crowns of my ancestors,
whose prayers sank in the holy stream.

A Love Song
by Else Lasker-Schüler

Out of golden breath
Heaven created us.
Oh, how we love one another.

Birds become buds on the branches
and roses flutter away.

I keep searching for your lips
behind a thousand kisses.

A night made of gold,
stars made of night—
no one can see us.

When daylight brings the green
we're slumbering—only our shoulders
still play like butterflies.

My Blue Piano
by Else Lasker-Schüler

At home I have a blue piano
but cannot play a single note.

It stands in the dark of the cellar door
ever since the world turned savage.

Four starry hands play,
the Moon Lady sang in her boat.
Now rats dance to a clatter.

Its keyboard is shattered—
I weep over the dead blue thing.

Ah dear Angel, I have eaten
such bitter bread—please open
for me while still alive—even
though forbidden—Heaven's door.

Exhausted, My Heart Rests
by Else Lasker-Schüler

Exhausted, my heart rests
on the night's velvet
and stars lie down on my eyelids.

I flow in the silver tones of an étude.
Am no more and yet am multiplied a thousand times—
spreading over our Earth: Peace.

I completed my life's final chord—
quietly fading away—as God intended:
A saving psalm—meant for the world to practice.

Young Girl
by Ricarda Huch

Swirling spring,
blossoming tree—
flames of youth leap up around her.
Untouched, her flowing skirts sweep by,
the leaves left by the years
decaying at her feet.

Fearless glance,
stormy stride into the midst
of the forest of danger.
Clash of weapons!
Beckoning song,
festive crowd with streaming hair.

Brave in battle,
lovely in dance,
unconcerned with fate or reward—
fortune keep you!
What crown will be yours one day,
oh Amazon.

VIII. IN THE PALACE OF CREATION

Lovers Quarrel

You were earth
and I was water.

You were abundant
and I danced over you.

When you disappeared
I grew deep,
dark as mystery.

Wild Music

You are playing your music again
and I run after each golden tone.

Suddenly I ring like a gong struck by God.
Oh, my heart is indestructible
whenever you play on it.

Strike me, Beloved, again and again.
Never stop sounding my wild thunder heart.

Revelations

I lift my head and gaze into your eyes.
A thunderbolt without beginning or end
pierces my heart.

Waves of the Mother—endless
tenderness—flood my lonely garden
with shocking bliss.

What is there to fear
when your smile
embraces every imaginable universe.

Your eyes,
huge shining pools,
deepen with obsidian mysteries.

One look from your Kali eye
evacuates whole destinies
of wrong—instantly.

Ah, petal by petal
You unfurl the flaring lotus
of my yearning heart.

Soft as milk,
clear as a mirror,
You are nearer than my Self.

Your eyes are golden
suns that pulsate
Yes! Yes! Yes!

You torch
the stubborn shell
around my seedling Self.

Your glance of honey
pulling me
into a web of incandescent Love.

You are the golden Lotus,
your petals woven from a million suns
blazing within.

Bubbling and gurgling
my heart pours joy.
You are always here.

Mira and Krishna

Mira sleeps in her grandfather's palace
and dreams of marrying Krishna.
Krishna grazes his cows by the flowing river.

Mira dances before his image waving oil lamps.
Krishna poises on the back
of a gold and black spotted snake.

Mira eats the meal her in-laws serve
with a cup of poison.
Krishna folds his legs into a lotus blossom.

Mira unbraids her hair, marks her brow with fiery color.
Krishna gazes under petaled brows,
dark curls on blue shoulders.

Mira takes the temple road,
the palace gate slams shut behind her.
Krishna snaps a reed and heaves a sigh of relief.

Mira is mad, they say, laughing, clapping.
Krishna dives off the serpent's back
into the deepest waters.

Mira grasps his foot
and spirals into the current.
Krishna's crocodile earring snags her swelling heart.

Mira is a pyre of aloe and sandalwood.
Krishna heats his long cool limbs
in her fragrant flames.

Mira sways in the crowd,
the universe circling her ankles.
Krishna sits in motionless contemplation.

Mira's heart is a wide open lily.
Krishna is the dusky breeze
that slashes her petals.

Mira tramps cross country begging, seeking.
Krishna plays his lilting flute
seated on her head.

Mira thirsts for every drop
yet suffocates in the mere aroma.
Krishna is beauty, the dazzling teacher.

Mira wrapped in a crimson sari
lights incense and opens her bed.
Krishna winks and vanishes.

Mira wide-eyed gnaws on love.
Krishna is a thorny bush
in the night never ending.

Mira grows proud and angry,
her senses greedy.
Krishna is the bottomless well of rage and grief.

Mira burns with fear and shame, doubt, disgust.
Krishna powders himself
with her silky ashes.

Mira beholds the circular saws
made for beheading.
Krishna's crown radiates diamonds and rubies.

Mira hears thunder, pounds her big drum.
Krishna, where are you? the peacock cries,
the lotus drowns in moonlight.

Mira rows on through tears,
her heart grown fat as a mango.
Krishna courses into the octopus oceans.

Mira balances a golden pitcher on her head.
Krishna overflows, flooding
the earth in green.

Mira hears footsteps
that mangle her heart with joy.
Krishna swings a rosary of perfect tears.

Mira unbolts the door, her white hair flowing.
Krishna's eyes are coppery clouds
with lightning.

Mira drenched in love
cries, *Darling!*
Krishna returns the love that is everlasting.

Mira takes his hand and rises out of her body.
Krishna plays a rapturous melody
upon it.

Mira's song spreads
to the farthest corners.
Krishna dances blissfully on the rim of the dark.

The Goddesses

Every living being is immortal,
says the first Goddess.
May demons not crouch on your chest,
says the second.
The eyes of the third Goddess well with tenderness.
The fourth radiates young life.
Very hard, utters the fifth.
More work to be done, says the sixth,
first sit in the sun.
The seventh delights,
Is your heart broken yet?
The eighth bursts with indignation.
The ninth will not judge.
The tenth Goddess cries, *I'm coming!*
The eleventh sighs, *There is nothing to be done.*
Beyond this pain, coos the twelfth,
are treasures.
Everything, proclaims the thirteenth Goddess,
is perfect as it is.

Mira is a pyre of aloe and sandalwood.
Krishna heats his long cool limbs
in her fragrant flames.

Mira sways in the crowd,
the universe circling her ankles.
Krishna sits in motionless contemplation.

Mira's heart is a wide open lily.
Krishna is the dusky breeze
that slashes her petals.

Mira tramps cross country begging, seeking.
Krishna plays his lilting flute
seated on her head.

Mira thirsts for every drop
yet suffocates in the mere aroma.
Krishna is beauty, the dazzling teacher.

Mira wrapped in a crimson sari
lights incense and opens her bed.
Krishna winks and vanishes.

Mira wide-eyed gnaws on love.
Krishna is a thorny bush
in the night never ending.

Mira grows proud and angry,
her senses greedy.
Krishna is the bottomless well of rage and grief.

Mira burns with fear and shame, doubt, disgust.
Krishna powders himself
with her silky ashes.

Mira beholds the circular saws
made for beheading.
Krishna's crown radiates diamonds and rubies.

Mira hears thunder, pounds her big drum.
Krishna, where are you? the peacock cries,
the lotus drowns in moonlight.

Mira rows on through tears,
her heart grown fat as a mango.
Krishna courses into the octopus oceans.

Mira balances a golden pitcher on her head.
Krishna overflows, flooding
the earth in green.

Mira hears footsteps
that mangle her heart with joy.
Krishna swings a rosary of perfect tears.

Mira unbolts the door, her white hair flowing.
Krishna's eyes are coppery clouds
with lightning.

Mira drenched in love
cries, *Darling!*
Krishna returns the love that is everlasting.

Mira takes his hand and rises out of her body.
Krishna plays a rapturous melody
upon it.

Mira's song spreads
to the farthest corners.
Krishna dances blissfully on the rim of the dark.

Scars Publications

Books

Sulphur & Sawdust
Slate & Marrow
Blister & Burn
Rinse & Repeat
Survive & Thrive
(not so) Warm & Fuzzy
Torture & Triumph
Oh.
the Elements
Infamous in our Prime
Anais Nin: an Understanding of her Art
the Electronic Windmill
Changing Woman
Harvest of Gems
the Little Monk
Death in Málaga
the Svetasvatara Upanishad
the Significance of the Frontier
the Swan Road
Momento Mori
IN THE PALACE OF CREATION
Hope Chest in the Attic
the Window
Close Cover Before Striking
Autumn Reason
(Woman.)
Contents Under Pressure
the Average Guy's Guide (to Feminism)
Changing Gears
The Key To Believing

Compact Discs

music

MFV the Demo Tapes
Kuypers the Final (*MFV Inclusive)*
Weeds & Flowers the Beauty & the Destruction
The Second Axing Something Is Sweating
Kuypers Overstating *voice sampling*
MFV, Weeds & Flowers, The Second Axing Stop. Look. Listen to the music
The Second Axing Live in Alaska *2 concerts*

audio art

Pettus/Kuypers Live at Cafe Aloha
Kuypers Seeing Things Differently
Pointless Orchestra Rough Mixes
Scars Torture & Triumph compilation CD
Kuypers Change/Rearrange
5D/5D Tick Tock
Scars Oh. web-based CD
Kuypers Six One One
Kuypers Stop. Look. Listen.
Order From Chaos The Entropy Project
Scars the Elements compilation CD
Kuypers Masterful Performances *mp3 CD*
Kuypers Death Comes in Threes

IN THE PALACE OF CREATION
first edition
ISBN#1-891470-43-4

http://scars.tv
Editor@scars.tv